FEARLESS COMPETITORS

LONGBOARD SKATEBOARDING

Enslow PUBLISHING

GAIL PARMAN

Please visit our website, www.enslow.com. For a free color catalog of all our high-quality books, call toll free 1-800-398-2504 or fax 1-877-980-4454

Published in 2027 by
Enslow Publishing
2544 Clinton Street
Buffalo, NY 14224

Portions of this work were originally authored by Peter Castellano and published as *Daredevil Sports: Longboard Skateboarding*. All new material in this edition is authored by Gail Parman.

Cataloging-in-Publication Data
Names: Parman, Gail.
Title: Longboard skateboarding / Gail Parman.
Description: Buffalo, NY : Enslow Publishing, 2027. | Series: Fearless competitors | Includes glossary and index.
Identifiers: ISBN 9781978548787 (pbk.) | ISBN 9781978548794 (library bound) | ISBN 9781978548800 (ebook)
Subjects: LCSH: Skateboarding--Juvenile literature.
Classification: LCC GV859.8 P377 2027 | DDC 796.22--dc23

Printed in China

Photos Credits: Cover, p. 1 AvokadoStudio/Shutterstock.com; p. 3 CapturePB/Shutterstock.com; p. 3, 4, 6, 8, 10, 12, 14, 17, 18, 20, 22, 24, 26, 28 (black background) Propakages/Shutterstock.com; p. 4 oneinchpunch/Shutterstock.com; p. 6 Library of Congress; p. 8 Will Rodrigues/Shutterstock.com; p. 10 Steve Collender/Shutterstock.com; p. 11 Ulrich Mueller/Shutterstock.com; p. 12 Eder Paisan/Shutterstock.com; p. 14 Divisual Jo/Shutterstock.com; p. 16 Sergei Bachlakov/Shutterstock.com; p. 18 Filippo Romanelli/Shutterstock.com; p. 20 Elena Shishkina/Shutterstock.com; p. 22 Marco Govel/Shutterstock.com; p. 24 Elena Yakusheva/Shutterstock.com; p. 26 Danylo Samiylenko/Shutterstock.com; p. 28 Yankovsky88/Shutterstock.com; p. 30 stockphoto-graf/Shutterstock.com

CPSIA compliance information: Batch #QSENS27: For further information, contact Enslow Publishing, New York, New York, at 1-800-398-2504.

Contents

THE NEED FOR SPEED

Skateboarding can be a high-speed sport. But what is a longboard? Longboard skateboards are longer and often wider than traditional skateboards. Many people ride a longboard to get around their neighborhood or city. There are many daring and exciting ways to ride a longboard too!

FEARLESS FACTS

The trick-heavy skateboarding most people know from the X Games and other TV **events** includes **vert** and street skateboarding. These don't usually use a longboard.

SKATEBOARDING BEGINS

Modern skateboarding started in the late 1940s, when surfers in California were looking for ways to practice their skills on land. The first skateboards were homemade, consisting of wooden boards with roller skate wheels attached to the bottom. Boards have changed a lot since then!

FEARLESS FACTS

Longboard surfing is similar to longboard skateboarding. Longboard surfboards are longer than the traditional boards, which usually makes them easier to paddle and catch waves.

By the early 1960s, skateboarding had evolved into its own sport, but concerns over safety grew. The wheels could slip and cause injury. In the 1970s, new, safer wheels led to renewed interest in skateboarding. Longer and wider skateboards, called longboards, were easier to control.

FEARLESS FACTS

The first skateboarding **competition** was held in 1963 in California. More than 100 people from across the U.S. competed.

GEAR UP!

All skateboards have three main parts that work together: the deck, the **trucks**, and the wheels. The deck, or the part the skater stands on, is longer and wider on a longboard than on a trick skateboard. Some longboards also have a stiffer deck, making it easier for the rider to balance.

FEARLESS FACTS

Longboard wheels are bigger and softer than those on trick skateboards. They make it easier to go fast and ride smoothly over bumpy ground.

Whether longboarding for travel or sport, all riders need to wear safety gear. Special helmets that fit well should always be worn, as well as knee and elbow pads and wrist guards. Some riders also choose to wear a mouth guard to keep their teeth protected.

FEARLESS FACTS

Skateboarders fall sometimes—even pros! Learn how to fall safely when you first start skating, especially if you plan on riding at high speeds.

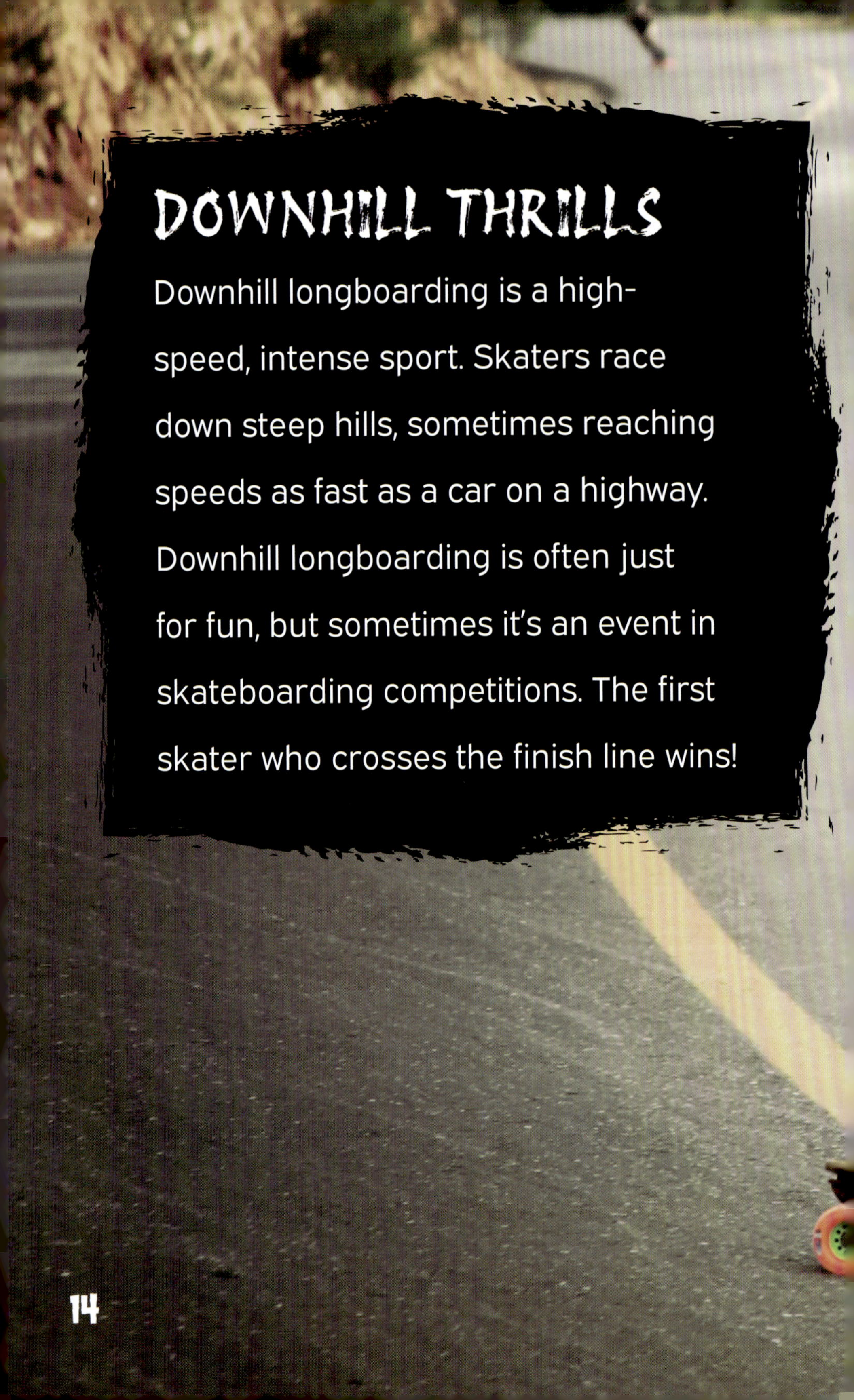

DOWNHILL THRILLS

Downhill longboarding is a high-speed, intense sport. Skaters race down steep hills, sometimes reaching speeds as fast as a car on a highway. Downhill longboarding is often just for fun, but sometimes it's an event in skateboarding competitions. The first skater who crosses the finish line wins!

FEARLESS FACTS

If you want to try downhill longboarding, ask an adult to help you and start with small hills. This dangerous sport requires commitment, bravery, and a lot of practice!

FEARLESS FACTS

Teutonia, Brazil, is famous for its downhill races. The track there is known as one of the scariest in the world—it's steep and fast, with rough roads that can make for a bumpy ride!

Downhill skateboarding is sometimes called a "**gravity** sport." Gravity sports, such as skiing and snowboarding, require the athlete to change their movements to use gravity to their advantage. In downhill skateboarding, riders position their bodies just right to reach top speeds!

THE RECORD BOOKS

Pete Connolly holds the record for the fastest longboard speed. In 2016, Pete had reached his fastest speed ever. But in 2017, he went even faster—and set a world record! He rode down a very steep hill in Québec, Canada, at 91 miles (147 km) per hour.

FEARLESS FACTS

Rob Thomson holds the world record for longest journey by skateboard. He rode across parts of Europe, the United States, and China on a longboard.

SKATE YOUR WAY

Skateboards are designed to be **versatile**. Longboards are traditionally used for cruising and downhill riding, but they can be ridden in lots of different ways. Some skaters carve, or lean right and left in an "S" shape, to stay in control.

FEARLESS FACTS

If you're doing tricks, that means you're freeriding. Skating around **obstacles**, or slaloming, is even more of a challenge!

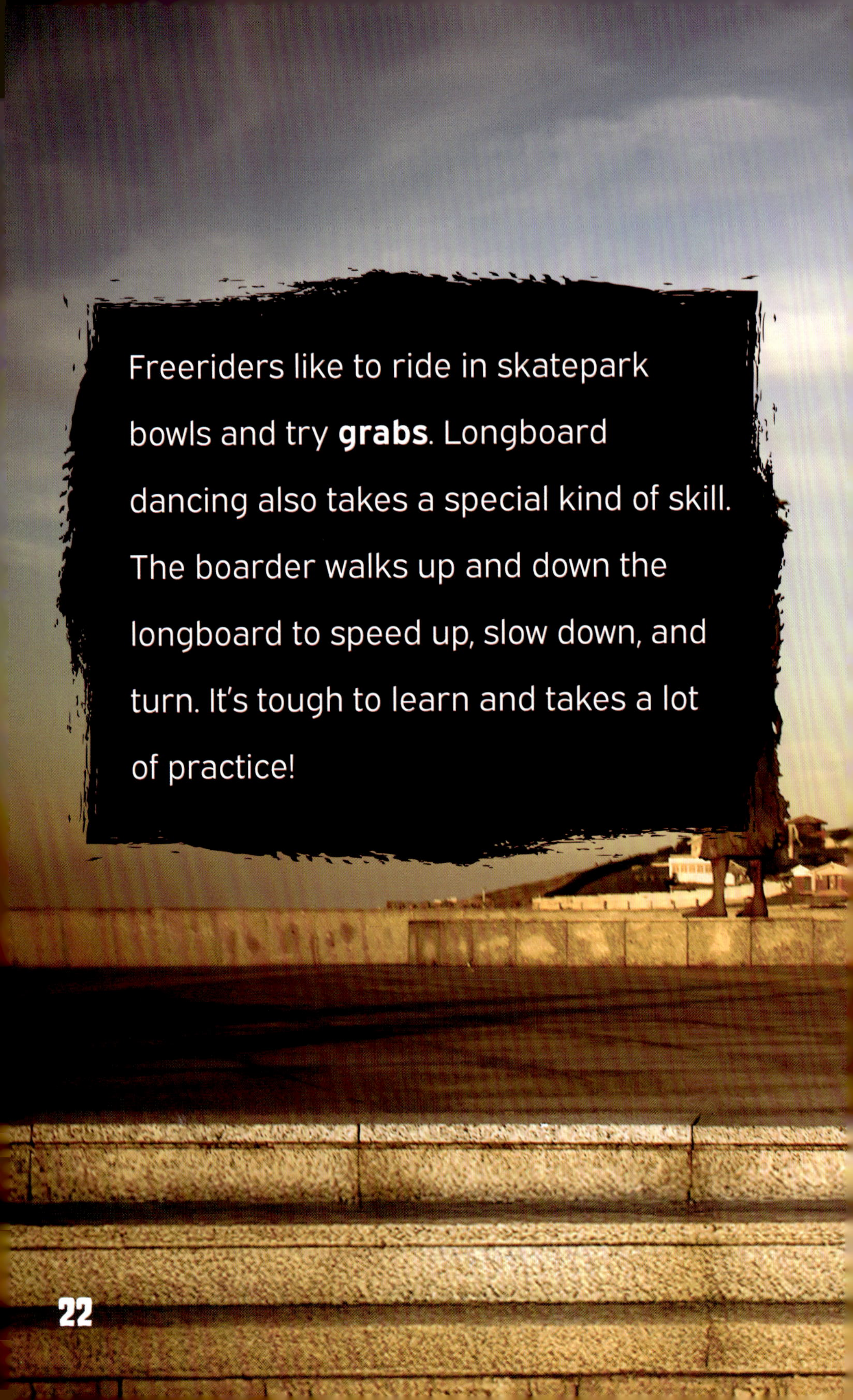

Freeriders like to ride in skatepark bowls and try **grabs**. Longboard dancing also takes a special kind of skill. The boarder walks up and down the longboard to speed up, slow down, and turn. It's tough to learn and takes a lot of practice!

FEARLESS FACTS

The longboard is a good choice for someone who wants to skateboard to get around. Some people even use them to get to school or work!

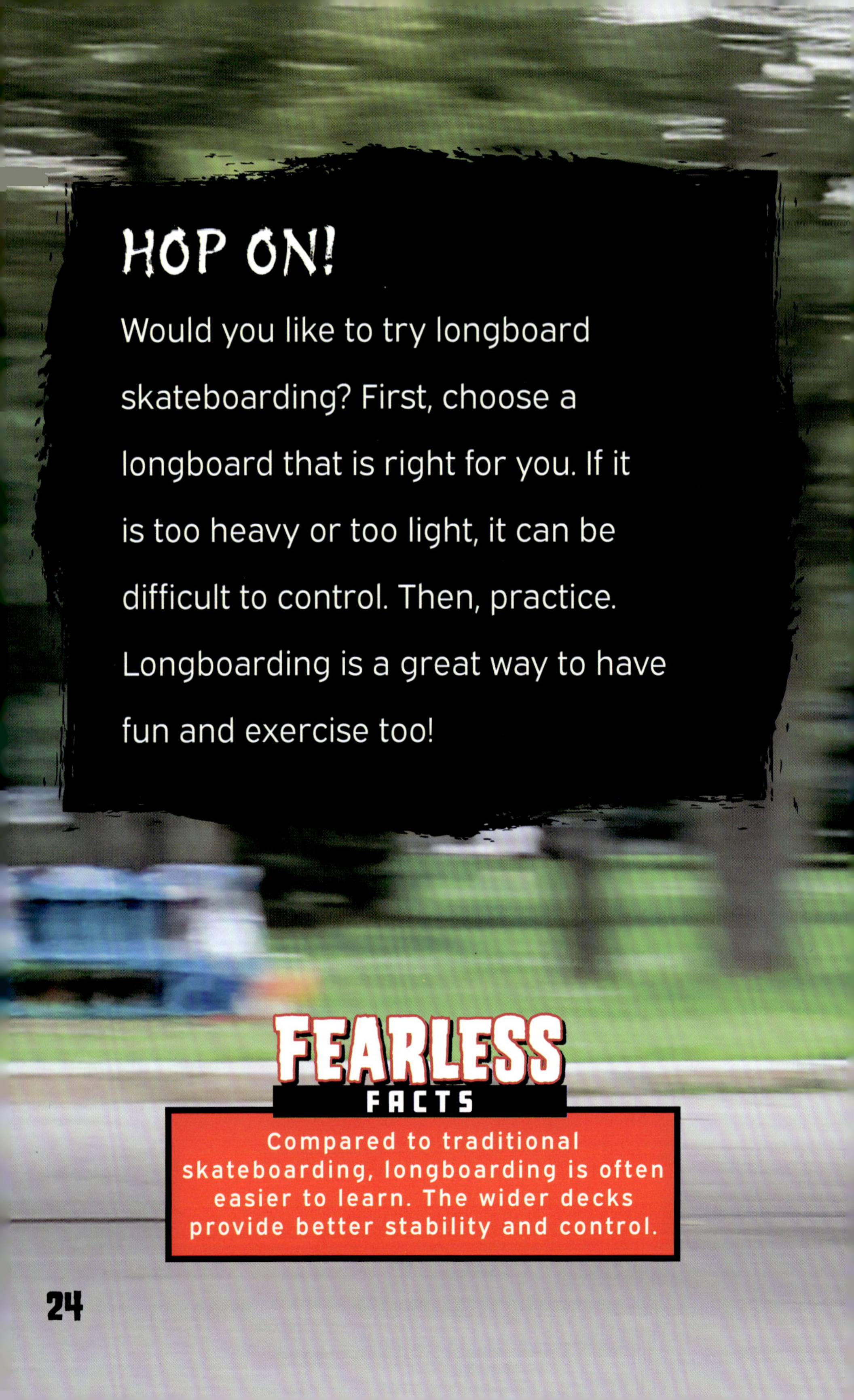

HOP ON!

Would you like to try longboard skateboarding? First, choose a longboard that is right for you. If it is too heavy or too light, it can be difficult to control. Then, practice. Longboarding is a great way to have fun and exercise too!

FEARLESS FACTS

Compared to traditional skateboarding, longboarding is often easier to learn. The wider decks provide better stability and control.

FOLLOW THE RULES

Longboarding is fun, but it can be dangerous. In some areas, it's even illegal! Police and government officials worry about the safety of skateboarders sharing the road with cars, especially when the riders are traveling at such fast speeds. A crash could be very dangerous!

FEARLESS FACTS

In West Vancouver, British Columbia, longboarders aren't supposed to ride on the hilly city streets. Cars not seeing boarders, or boarders zooming through stoplights, have caused many serious car accidents.

NO
SKATEBOARDING
SKATING OR
BICYCLING
BEYOND THIS
POINT

PICKING UP SPEED

Longboarding has evolved from a hobby to a mainstream sport, and it shows no signs of slowing down. New, creative ways of riding are sure to come. So, grab a helmet and some knee pads and hop on!

FEARLESS FACTS

An important skill for every longboarder to learn is how to brake. The basic method is to lightly drag your back foot along the ground to slow down safely. But even this takes practice!

Safety First

ALL LONGBOARD SKATEBOARDERS SHOULD:

- wear a helmet, knee pads, elbow pads, and other safety gear.
- keep their board in good shape and check it for problems before using it.
- follow traffic laws to keep out of cars' way.
- know their skill level—some tricks and uneven ground will be too hard for beginners.
- do other forms of exercise, such as running and playing sports, to stay injury-free.
- avoid riding at night or in wet or icy weather.

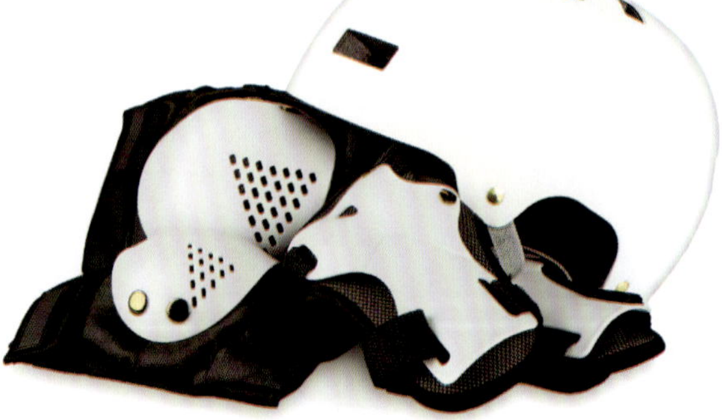

For More Information

BOOKS

Morey, Allan. *Skateboarding*. Black Rabbit Books, 2024.

Murray, Julie. *Skateboarding*. Abdo Kids, 2023.

Towler, Paige. *Skateboards: The Cool Stories and Facts Behind Every Trick*. Union Square Kids, 2024.

WEBSITES

Longboarding Facts for Kids

https://kids.kiddle.co/Longboarding

Take a look at more fun facts about longboarding and learn some of the lingo!

Skateboarding

https://kids.britannica.com/kids/article/skateboarding/437407

Britannica Kids shares information about the history of skateboarding and its impact on our culture.

Glossary

competition: a contest someone tries to win

event: a happening

grab: a skateboarding trick in which the skateboarder grabs the side of the board while in the air

gravity: the force that pulls objects toward Earth's center

obstacle: something that blocks a path

truck: the T-shaped piece of metal that attaches a skateboard wheel to the underside of the deck

versatile: able to be used in many different ways

vert: short for "vertical," an event in skateboarding involving a ramp and the skateboarder changing from horizontal movement to vertical movement to do a trick

Index